EXTREME MATH

EXTREME MATH

RealMath
RealPeople
RealSports

KipTyler & **Marya**WashingtonTyler

PRUFROCK PRESS, INC.
P.O. Box 8813
Waco, TX 76714-8813
Phone: (800) 998-2208
Fax: (800) 240-0333
www.prufrock.com

Contents

Extreme Sports
Extreme Math

At first glance, mathematics and extreme sports are at opposite extremes. There is no multiplying or dividing in bronco riding or hang gliding, is there? Certainly no one kayaking through a foaming whirlpool of whitewater has any interest in the pluses and minuses of math, do they?

In fact, math and the extreme sports have a lot in common. Those who venture into extreme sports seek the outer limits of their potential. They face the unknown and gain courage as they overcome their fears. There is no failure except fear.

Math, too, is a daring pursuit of the unknown. Go seeking answers, and you will find them. The journey beckons …

1 E. J. Jackson
Freestyle Kayaker

Following directions
Averaging two numbers

The "hole" in a whitewater river is an 8-feet-deep, churning chaos of water and foam that would strike fear into the heart of any ordinary person. Freestyle kayakers like World Champion E. J. Jackson revel in holes! They compete to see who can keep their kayak positioned right in the middle of the hole without being sucked under its powerful current, and style counts. They earn extra points for doing tricks in the hole, too, but one false move and the whirlpool sucks them under, whips them up like a blender, and spits them out somewhere down the river.

The scoring system, developed by the competitors themselves may be almost as complicated as the sport is difficult. Want to try it?

Technical Points

First, you can get technical points by spinning your boat around. Every time your boat spins halfway (180 degrees), you get one point. Turn all the way around (360 degrees), and you get two points.

If you get either end of the kayak to nose up out of the water while you are turning (we call this "elevation"), you get more points:

flat-45-degree angle	1 point
45–70-degree angle	2 points
70–110-degree angle	4 points

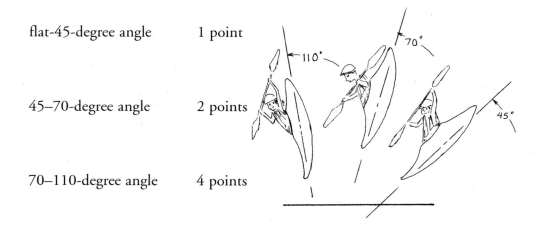

Everything happens so fast that the four judges don't always agree, so after totaling each judge's scores, the highest score given and the lowest score given are thrown out. The two remaining technical scores are added together. This number is called the multiplier.

Try this. You stay in the hole the full 30 seconds, and in the process spin your boat completely around several times.

Judge #1 gives you 10 technical points.
Judge #2 gives you 15 technical points.
Judge #3 gives you 7 technical points.
Judge #4 gives you 10 technical points.

1. What's the multiplier?

Variety Points

Variety points are awarded for each new trick you do while you're spinning (e.g., if you turn the kayak on end). Again, the high and low scores are thrown out, and this time we take the average. Then we add one (which is done so that no one competing will ever get a zero).

For example:

Judge #1 awards 1 variety point.
Judge #2 awards 2 variety points.
Judge #3 awards 3 variety points.
Judge #4 awards 5 variety points.

2.   Find the Variety Points score.

3.   Now multiply the Technical Score (the multiplier) times the Variety Points.

Style Bonus Points

We're not done yet. (Freestyle kayakers must *really* like math.) Each judge also awards style bonus points, and this time we use the average between the two middle judges. Then, that number is turned into a percent and multiplied times the answer that you figured out above and added on. We'll help you.

Let's say the four style judges give you a 7, 8, 13, and 10.

4.   Discarding the high and low, what was your average?

5.   Take that % of 70.

6.   Add this to the previous answer to get your total score.

"Winners in life conquer their fears."

As you see, if you plan on becoming a world champion kayaker, you need math. E. J. travels extensively, hon-

"The way to determine whether a fear is justified is to determine the calculated risk." E. J. Jackson

ing his skills on rivers throughout the world. Everywhere he travels, his wife and two children accompany him.

"One of my dad's favorite quotes is by Albert Einstein. 'He who conquers fear and doubt, conquers failure.' I like that." Emily (E. J.'s 11-year-old daughter)

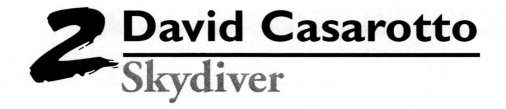 David Casarotto
Skydiver

Reading tables
Converting miles to feet, hours to seconds
Multistep problem solving
Large number division
Cross-multiplying fractions
Negative numbers and temperatures

What does it feel like to dive out of an airplane? David Casarotto, who has over 800 dives to his credit, describes it like this:

"Imagine what it feels like to lean your head out of the car window when the car is traveling down the highway at 60 miles per hour. Now imagine what it feels like sticking your head out of a plane traveling at 100 miles per hour, getting ready to jump 18,000 feet above the ground."

Leaving the Plane

"Skydiving is not a sensation of falling. The first few seconds you are recovering from the forward momentum when you were on the plane, and you're going sideways as well as down.

"Then, you begin falling downward, and you fall faster and faster and faster until finally you're going as fast as you could go against the resistance of air (terminal velocity). All of this happens in the first 9 seconds."

1. Look at the table on the next page. How far did David fall in the first second?

Time Since Leaving Plane	Total Length of Fall
1 sec	16 ft
2 sec	62 ft
3 sec	138 ft
6 sec	500 ft
9 sec	1,028 ft
12 sec	1,556 ft
15 sec	2,084 ft

2. **How far did David fall between the first second and the second second?**

3. **How far did he fall in the first 9 seconds?**

Freefall

You're in freefall, engulfed in brain-chilling wind, falling at 120 miles per hour.

4. **How many miles are you falling every minute?**

5. **How many seconds will it take you to fall 1 mile?**

6. **How many feet are you falling each second? (Hint: There are 5,280 feet in a mile.)**

"Leaving a plane going 100 miles an hour is just like leaving a car being driven at 100 miles per hour. The difference between jumping out of a plane and jumping out of a car, of course, is that you have a lot more time to enjoy the scenery on the way down." David Casarotto

David doesn't think much of the new craze to speed sky-dive. He says, "In a normal freefall you are lying in a flat position, but in a speed fall you are headfirst, which means much less air resistance. Headfirst you can fall at 240 miles per hour! The potential for serious injury is much greater."

7.   In a headfirst speed dive, how many feet per second does a person approach the ground?

Opening Shock

David continues, "Now, there's the deployment of the parachute. When you open your parachute, the speed of your fall is suddenly cut drastically, and the shock to your body is tremendous. In just 3 seconds, even in the normal jump position, your downward speed changes from 176 feet per second to only 20 feet per second. The change is so drastic that if you didn't have leg straps as well as shoulder straps attaching you to the parachute, you would break through the harness and that would be the last jump you ever made.

For those 3 seconds, you are experiencing 10g, which means you are experiencing 10 times the normal pull of gravity on your body."

David weighs approximately 180 pounds; his helmet and harness together weigh about 20 pounds; and, if he is carrying oxygen, his tank weighs another 5 pounds. When David pulls the ripcord to deploy his parachute, he experiences all this weight times 10.

8.   How much weight is David experiencing?

In Flight

David uses two parachutes. When David is using his raspberry-colored parachute, he has a rate of descent at about 25 feet/second. When he is using his lime green parachute, David has a rate of descent of at least 40 feet/second. The raspberry parachute has an area of 150 square feet. The lime green parachute has an area of 107 square feet.

David usually deploys the parachute about 3,000 feet above the ground.

9. How many seconds does David have after deployment of the raspberry parachute until he hits the ground?

10. How many seconds does David have after deployment of the lime green parachute until he hits the ground?

Touching Down

"Oh, yes. And then there's landing. That's the easy part. If properly executed, it's like stepping off a small stool."

More Stuff You Might Want to Know

Sometimes David jumps with a group of other divers and they all fall in a formation such as a circle or a star, holding on to each other's hands or feet. In these dives, David carries an audible altimeter under his helmet that warns him to break away when he is approaching the ground.

11. David is freefalling in a group at 165 feet per second. At 4,000 feet, he hears the altimeter warn him to break off soon. About how many seconds until he reaches 3,000 feet, when he must deploy his parachute?

Take it from David, "One of the hardest things about skydiving is the extreme cold. For every 1,000 feet of altitude gained, there is a loss of 3 degrees Fahrenheit. Add to that the extreme wind chill, and you're facing some incredible frigid cold."

"Actually, the body heats up during free fall—because of the friction I suppose, and because of the adrenaline rushing through your system. It's mostly your hands that suffer. Your hands go numb with the cold." David Casarotto

David's highest jump was from an airplane flying at 18,000 feet above the ground. (That's so high he had to bring his own oxygen.)

12. If the temperature on the ground was a pleasant 50 degrees Fahrenheit, what was the temperature up there (not counting wind chill)?

Is It Too Dangerous?

"There's an inherent danger with all of it. I'd be crazy not to admit that. I've had my canopy and another person's get entangled. I've broken suspension lines. Twice I've had a suspension line end up over the canopy, preventing the parachute from inflating. Each time, the emergency parachute saved me."

So why does David keep going up? "It's kind of in your blood after awhile. It's not something you can turn off. But believe me, I dot my i's. I cross my t's. I keep my gear in top condition. I do everything I can to be safe. I've never not walked away from a fall, and I intend to keep it that way."

3 James Cole
Bronco Rider

Multiplication of decimals
Rounding
Multistep problem solving
Finding a pattern

If you can stay on for 8 seconds you're good. If you can do it with style, you're a champion.

What's it like riding a bucking, writhing tornado of a horse that wants nothing more than to flip you off his back, turn you upside down, and step on you? Ask James Cole of Red Lodge, MT, National High School Saddle Bronc Riding Champion. James started bronc riding when he was 14, and in the last 4 years has endured a broken toe, a bruised kidney, and two separated shoulders. You could say he's gotten off relatively easy for this sport.

In a bronc riding competition, finalists are given just one ride—one chance to stay on the wildest, meanest, most untamed horse in the territory. Attendants hold the frightened horse in a closed pen while the rider mounts. James wraps his hand around the leather strap, nods his head, and, in one critical second, the attendant yanks the horse's underbelly strap tight and the gate opens. The bronco, enraged by the tightness, embarks on a bucking, twisting, leaping, rearing rampage. It will only last 8 seconds, even less if the rider is thrown off; but, in this business, 8 seconds is a very long time.

"You don't hear or feel anything when you're riding," James explains. "As soon as you nod your head that you're ready, you don't hear or feel or even think anything until it's over."

James hopes in every bronc riding competition that luck will give him the meanest, toughest horse in the corral. If the horse doesn't put up enough of a fight, it can hurt the rider's chances of qualifying. A really tough horse can earn up to 25 points. A really tough rider, by staying calm and in complete control, can also earn up to 25 points. At the largest rodeo in the world, the National High School Rodeo Finals with well over 1,000 riders in competition, James walked away with the grand prize. It was his first time in national competition.

James intends to stay involved with the sport for the rest of his life, but he doesn't recommend bronco riding for most people. "Even if you do it right," he says, "it hurts."

Here is a sampling of the math that James encounters while on the rodeo circuit:

1. **"In order to enter a certain rodeo, each contestant has to pay a fee of $50.00, $7.00 of which is used to pay for the animals brought in and $3.00 of which goes to pay the judges. One hundred dollars extra has been donated to the pot by an unidentified source. I am one of 20 contestants entered. First place will win 60% of the pot."**

   What do I get if I win?

2. **What is rodeo life like? "You do a lot of traveling. I went to three rodeos last weekend and traveled over 1,000 miles."**

"Here's a problem for you. Let's say three of my buddies and I are off to a rodeo 125 miles away. Let's say gas costs $1.70 per gallon and the car averages 32 miles per gallon."

How much should each one of us contribute for gas for the round trip?

3.   **"At the finals, all contestants ride twice to determine the top riders. The top riders advance to the one-ride "short go" round. We compete under a point system where first place earns 10 points, second place gets 9 points, third place gets 8 points, etc."**

Contestant	First Go	Second Go	Short Go
Tornado Joe	58	62	68
Danny Daniels	68	60	58
Wild Willy	70	52	56
Jamers	65	70	69
Oscar	64	56	70
Blaze	72	66	54
Goose-Egg	69	50	72
Tarzan	67	54	67

In the first go, the contestant who calls himself Blaze and his horse received the highest score, so Blaze gets 10 points. Wild Willy gets 9 points for coming in second. I got 5 points for coming in fifth.

4. Figure the overall winner. Who has the most
total points?

4 Juli Lynch
Adventure Racer

Reading a topographic map
Measurement and scale
Multiplying by decimals
Dividing by decimals
Adding fractions/Rounding

Your team of five is racing in the Eco-Challenge. It is 2 a.m. You have arrived at the summit of a 19,000-foot volcano. All of you are expert climbers, but one of you has developed a painful knee. It has been snowing. With the wind chill, it is below zero. There is a mist; it is damp. Some of you are cold.

You climb down the other side of the volcano and head into the forest. There is no trail—nothing but slippery rocks, waist-high fallen trees blocking your route in every direction, and mud, sometimes knee-deep. You travel without sleep and continue racing through the long dark night. It's easy to get lost.

At last you make it to the river and it takes an hour to find your team's canoes. You hope to gain some time by paddling with every ounce of your strength. You cover more than 70 miles, ditch the canoes, and set off on a 50-mile run. The run takes your team across a dried-up lakebed, and the temperature is now reading 140 degrees (F) with no shade. And, oh, by the way—there is no water either.

This is fun. This is adventure racing.

"Adventure racing is about endurance. Adventure racers test themselves to the limits of endurance, and, in the process, they find out they can do more than they ever thought possible." Juli Lynch

Adventure racers cover extreme distances across extreme terrain under extreme conditions. Adventure racing might be considered the most extreme of the extreme sports, and Juli Lynch is one of the best in the world.

"Winning is not my only focus. I focus on finishing. There are far more lessons you can learn by staying in the race—no matter where you finish—than by quitting because you don't think you'll win." Juli Lynch

Juli has skied across whole countries, waded through crocodile-infested waters, scaled sheer vertical cliffs, and slogged for miles through waist-deep mud carrying her bicycle on her shoulders. Juli has rafted, run, climbed, skied, swum, bushwhacked, mountain-biked, waded, and horseback-ridden across the remotest sections of countries like Mexico, Australia, Ecuador, Finland, and Argentina. She has drunk from parasite-infested waters, lived off moldy food, slept in the mud, and sometimes struggled on for days without food and water. This kind of extreme struggle is what adventure racers do—the ones who don't quit, that is.

Challenge #1

No time to lose. Let's get ready. We'll need water and plenty of it, plus a pump for filtering any water we might find in streams or lakes

"It is not unusual for me to lose up to 10 pounds in those long races." Juli Lynch

along the way. And we'll need food … lots of it. An average person going to work or school uses about 1,500 calories a day, but an adventure racer can burn 10,000 calories a day or more!

1. **In an adventure race, how many calories might you need each hour?** (Figure to the nearest calorie.)

Food is fuel—that's the battle cry for the adventure racer. There are three kinds of fuel: carbohydrates, protein, and fat. **Carbohydrates**, like breads, cereals, fruit, vegetables, and sugars, keep an adventure racer going. Without a continuous supply of carbohydrate energy, the athlete *bonks* (which means he or she can't go on).

> "I apply much of what I have learned from adventure racing to my everyday life." Juli Lynch

2. **Seventy-five percent of a racer's calories should consist of carbohydrates. How many carbohydrate calories will you consume in a full-speed race day?** (Figure to the nearest calorie.)

3. **Each gram of carbohydrate is equal to 4 calories. How many grams of carbohydrates should we take per person per day?**

We also need **protein**, like milk, yogurt, eggs, meat, fish, and beans. Protein heals tired and overworked muscles and fixes injuries. Without it, the long days and nights without rest will catch up, resulting in injury. Your daily protein needs while racing will be equal to your body weight in kg x 1.6g of protein.

> "The best foods for an adventure racer have a lot of calories, but don't weigh much. Cans of sardines and tuna sound delicious to most adventure racers craving protein and fat, but they are just too heavy to carry." Juli Lynch

4. **If you weigh 100 pounds, what is your weight in kilograms? Hint: 1 kilogram = 2.2 pounds**
   0.45 kilogram = 1 pound
   (Figure to the nearest kilogram.)

5. How many grams of protein would you need to take for each day of the race if you weigh 100 pounds? (Figure to the nearest kilogram.)

We also need **fat**—the best kinds are fish oils, vegetable oils, and nuts. Fat is needed as the slow-burning fuel, particularly when the weather is cold. Each gram of fat contains 9 calories.

"The hardest part about racing is the lack of fresh fruits and vegetables." Juli Lynch

6. If you need to eat 1,000 calories of fat for each day of a 6-day race, how many grams of fat should you pack? (Figure to the nearest gram.)

Challenge #2

Okay, your team has gathered here at the start, and the race begins in a half hour. The location of the finish line has just now been revealed, so your team can begin to plan your route. Look at the topographic map provided. Figure out the fastest, safest, shortest route to the first check point. A wrong choice will add hours and even days to your trek and is sure to make life miserable along the way.

Let's start by estimating the distance of each possible route. Here's how Juli does it. "Use a piece of string, place it along the route, and then compare it to the scale at the bottom of the map."

Measure each to the nearest ten kilometers.

7. Estimated Distance of Route A:

8. Estimated Distance of Route B:

9. Estimated Distance of Route C:

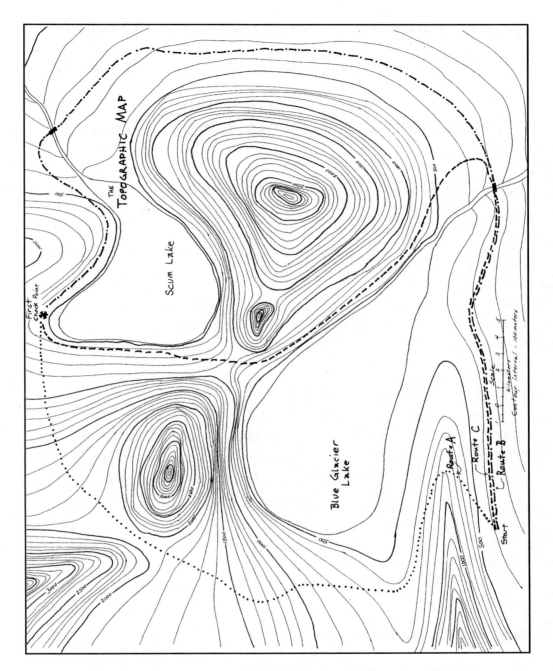

Let's figure how long each route would take.

Adventure racers run level trails and roads at about 8 kilometers per hour (5 miles per hour). If that doesn't sound very fast, remember adventure racers are carrying heavy backpacks on their backs for days and have been traveling with little or no sleep.

Calculate each of these to the nearest half hour. Round up when in the middle.

10. How long will it take to complete Route A?

11. How long will it take to complete Route B?

12. How long will it take to complete Route C?

Now you know which way is the shortest, but is the shortest way always the fastest? Not if the shortest way is straight up!

Fortunately, the topographic map has contour lines to compare elevations. Contour lines will help you find the flattest, and hopefully easiest, way to get there.

Follow one contour line with your pencil. If you walk that contour line, your route will be flat, and it will always be the same height above sea level. The contour lines next to that line are either 100 meters uphill or 100 meters downhill.

Hints:
1) Where the lines are close together, the land is steeper. Where the lines are far apart, it is flatter.
2) If a contour line makes a circle, it means a mountain or hill.

Count the contour lines crossed by each route; don't count the downhill parts. Then, figure how much you would have to climb (your elevation gain).

Figure to the nearest 100 meters:

13. Elevation gain of Route A: _____ m

14. Elevation gain of Route B: _____ m

15. Elevation gain of Route C: _____ m

Well, all that uphill climbing takes a bit longer, of course. For every 300 meters of elevation gain, add an hour to the expected time.

Figure these times to the nearest half-hour.

16. Hours to complete Route **A** considering elevation gain.

17. Hours to complete Route **B** considering elevation gain.

18. Hours to complete Route **C** considering elevation gain.

Still can't decide? See Challenge #3.

Challenge #3

The real map of what you will face is on the next page. You know, based on distance and elevation, how long each of the routes are expected to take. However, real life sometimes throws in surprises … and that's especially true in adventure racing. Pick a route.

Juli Lynch has been adventure racing since 1995 and has competed in international races such as the Raid Gauloises, the ESPN Extreme Games, and the Eco-Challenge. She is a contributing author to *The Complete Adventure Racing Book*.

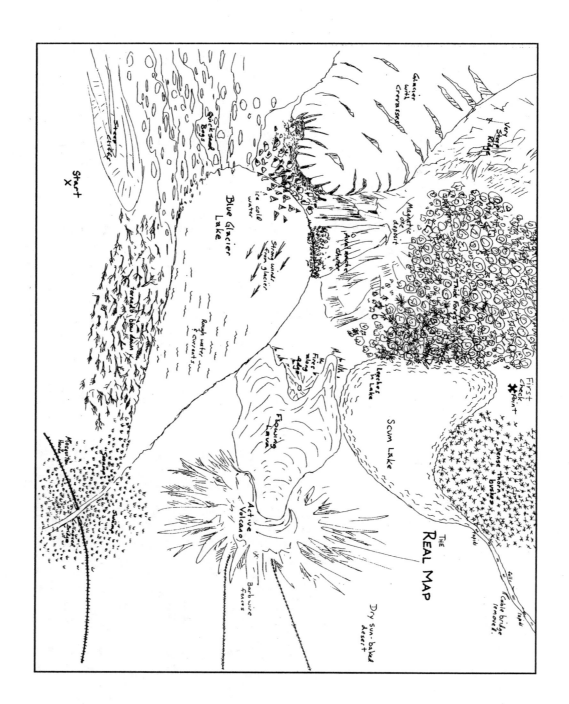

5 Jamie Simon
Freestyle Kayaker

Changing meters to feet
Multiplying/dividing by decimals

Imagine paddling your kayak into the middle of a whirlpool—for fun.

Have you ever heard of a hydraulic? It's a place where the water gushes over a boulder and flows back on itself—an upended whirlpool. Freestyle kayakers take pleasure in being sucked around in hydraulics and being spit out like watermelon seeds on the other side. Some even dare to perform tricks in the chaotic turmoil of waters—doing blunts, roundhouses, pirouettes, and even cartwheels! Yes, even cartwheels—using the force of the water to turn their kayaks end over end in the middle of the foaming turbulence.

Sound crazy? Actually, the worst danger in freestyle kayaking is usually a pulled muscle or a dislocated shoulder. However, kayakers don't become skilled without plenty of river experience, and any time you're on a whitewater river, danger is present.

Once, a hydraulic brought Jamie Simon, the world female freestyle kayak champion, closer to death than she ever wants to come again. "The water was really big—10 times its normal size—and my kayak was pulled underwater to the bottom of a hydraulic. My helmet was sucked off, and all the wind was knocked out of me. I couldn't paddle. Next thing I knew, I was carried over a class VI rapids." "Still," says Jamie, "I lived through it. It was the scariest thing that ever happened to me."

Freestyle kayakers like Jamie use plenty of math. "When we travel, a lot of times we need to figure out the average drop of the river. Say we put in at a town here and plan to take out at a cornfield down river. We are told that in the 7 miles between,

the river drops 2,750 feet. We know that there is 1 mile along this section with a drop of 500 feet, but we need to figure out what to expect in terms of average drop per mile for the rest of the route."

1. Help Jamie calculate the average drop for the rest of the route.

Jamie is one of the few kayakers alive to have run Hollin (pronounced Hoyin) Falls in Ecuador. Before she went to Ecuador, she read

that Hollin Falls is about 15 meters high, but what does 15 meters look like?

"It's easier for me to visualize in feet. This happens to me a lot—I'll be in another country, and when I ask how high the waterfalls on the river are, the people will tell me in meters. Then, I have to convert to feet in order to visualize them."

Almost every country except the United States and Great Britain use the metric system. So, how can you convert? Here's a hint. *Webster's Dictionary's* "Table of Weights and Measures" tells us that 1 yard = 0.914 meters.

2. How many feet high is Hollin Falls? Round to the nearest foot.

3. How many times taller is Hollin Falls than the ceiling in this room?

6 Jeff Gildehaus
Hang Glider

Using and comparing rates
Making a chart and graph
Division, rounding
Finding, using information
Extraneous information

Jeff Gildehaus is a master-rated hang glider pilot, one of only 200 in the world.

"I was always on the lookout for aircraft when I was growing up. My parents had a tough time getting past an airport without me wanting to watch at least one take-off or landing.

"The first time I saw a hang glider fly, I was 15. There is no engine noise with hang gliders because they have no engines. They simply glide. Gliding looked like so much fun that I knew right then I wanted to try it. By the time I was 16, I had saved up enough money bussing tables after school to buy my first hang glider. It was a Chandelle 16-foot standard rogallo with 160 square feet of sail area. It cost me $500 for the glider, harness, and five lessons.

"I named my glider Fletcher. The glider had a glide ratio of 4:1, meaning I could glide ahead 4 feet for every foot of altitude I fell. It also had a stall speed of 15 mph, a sink rate of 250 feet/minute, and a maximum speed of 35 mph. It was considered state-of-the-art at the time.

The hang glider I fly in today is a Moyes Xtra-lite with 147 square feet of sail area. I named it Barney. (It's purple and green.) Other than the aluminum air-craft tubing and Dacron sailcloth, there isn't much similarity between Barney and Fletcher. The Xtra-lite has a glide ratio of 13:1, a sink rate of 170 feet/minute, a stall speed of 17 mph, and can attain speeds of over 50 mph."

1. **Prepare a chart comparing statistics on the two hang gliders.**

Name of Glider	Sail Area	Glide Ratio	Sink Rate	Stall Speed	Max Speed

2. **"If I were to take off from a cliff with 1,000 feet of vertical drop between the launch and the landing area in my first hang glider, Fletcher, and then in my current hang glider, Barney, how much farther would I glide in Barney?"**

3. **"How long would I be able to stay in the air with Fletcher assuming there was no wind to extend the flight?"** (This is where sink rate becomes important.)

4. **"How long would I be able to stay in the air with Barney assuming there was no wind to extend the flight?"** (Round to the nearest whole number.)

Jeff continues, "Have you ever walked barefoot across a parking lot in the summertime? It can get hot, even though the lawn might feel cool. Different parts of the earth's surface have different heat absorption rates, and this difference causes rising air currents called 'thermals'.

"I like thermals. Thermal lift can take a hang glider all the way up to the clouds. In the flight that resulted in my greatest altitude gain ever, the thermal lift was so strong and wide that I couldn't get down! I had taken off from Steamboat in Colorado at 9,000 feet above mean sea level (msl), found a thermal, and climbed to 12,000 feet msl in 6 minutes. I flew around for 5 minutes before I found another thermal and started to climb rapidly at about 1,000 feet/minute. Soon I was at 16,000 msl and tried to level out, but I couldn't stop the glider from climbing, even as I put the nose down and pushed my speed up to 50 mph!

"I was being lifted skyward by a big one! I flew straight ahead in a full dive to try to get to the edge of the cloud before the lift could take me inside. I made it to the edge just as I reached the cloud base at 20,000 msl! I gained another 1,500 feet up the side of the cloud before I was far enough away to get out of the lift. Then, finally, 19 minutes after takeoff, I began to work my way back down. The past few minutes had seemed like an eternity. I took a good long time to get below 16,000 msl, and I had a total flight time of 1 hour 45 minutes when I set down in the landing area at 7,700 msl."

5. **"Draw a line on the chart showing my approximate elevation over the first 20 minutes."**

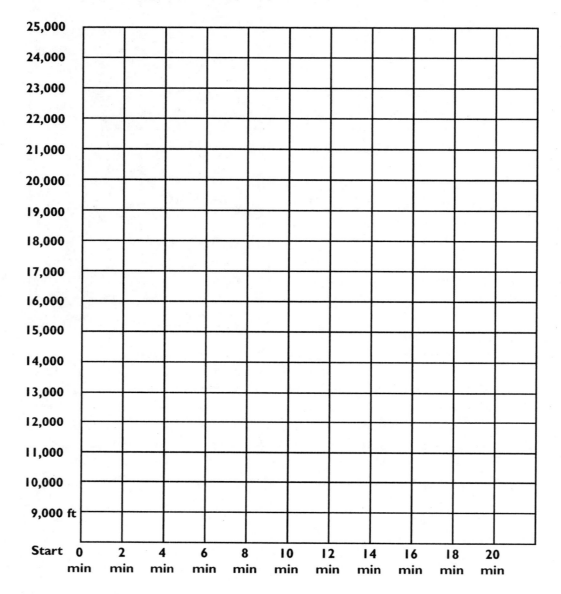

6. **"What was my rate of climb the first 6 minutes of the flight?"**

7. **"What was my rate of climb from 11 minutes to 19 minutes?"** Round to the nearest whole number.

"That was my highest flight. My longest flight also used thermals. I took off from at 6,000 msl near Dinosaur, CO. I circled around in weak thermals for 45 minutes before getting a strong enough thermal to climb to 15,000 msl and head out cross-country. My goal was to fly as far as I could toward my house, 131 miles away.

I had a nice flight of 15 miles before I was back down to 6,500 msl and decided I had better get ready to land. I was setting up my final approach at 6,300 msl (100 feet above the ground) when I flew into another thermal. I was able to climb back up to cloud base at 17,000 msl and keep going! I stayed between 15,000 msl and 18,000 msl for the next 60 miles before the series of clouds (we call it a cloud street) ended. I landed in a pasture next to the highway 100 miles from where I'd launched, and I'd been in the air for 4 hours and 45 minutes. While this is my best flight, it's not even close to the world record of 435 miles by Manfred Ruhmer in 10 hours 30 minutes!"

8. "How much longer was Manfred's flight distance than mine?"

9. "How much longer was Manfred's flight time than mine?"

10. "What was my average speed over the ground on my cross-country flight?" (Don't count the first 45 minutes of circling.)

11. "What was Manfred's average speed to the nearest whole number?"

12. **"How long would it have taken me to get home if I had been able to fly as fast as Manfred Ruhmer?"** Calculate to nearest half-hour.

7 The Braun Family
Polar Bear Swimmers

Finding volume in cubic inches
Dividing by decimals
Too much information
Rounding decimals

It is January 1st in the Wisconsin north woods. The air temperature is -4 degrees F, but with wind chill it's 20 below. Spectators line the frozen lakeshore, bundled in fur hats, down parkas, and fuzzy mittens ... shivering. The roar of chain-saws fills the air as event organizers undertake the task of opening a hole in the foot-thick lake ice. While the huge blocks are cut and laboriously heaved upon the frozen surface, two young men, Scott and Stan, and their middle-aged mother, Connie, wait by the bonfire in flip-flops and cotton bathrobes, locked in sober meditation. They are preparing to go swimming.

Polar bear swimming may not be an actual sport, but it certainly is extreme. Normal swimming water temperature is about 90 degrees Fahrenheit. People will complain if a recreational swimming pool is colder than 80 degrees. But, when water has formed ice on top, you know its tem-

"The first half of the swim you're thinking, 'This ain't bad,' then all of a sudden, it hits you just how stupid this is." Stan Braun

"It's actually refreshing. It's definitely exhilarating." Scott Braun

perature is below 32. Cold water swimming is not an endeavor to be taken lightly, nor under any circumstances should it be tried without safe supervision.

Scott and Stan began this polar bear swim event 10 years ago because they had a list of things they wanted to do before they became too old. Polar bear swimming was one thing, as was running a marathon, skydiving, fire walking, and bungee jumping. They have done them all. According to Stan, "We used to do this just to be crazy. Now, we are doing it for charity." This year's entry fees brought in over $10,000 for Big Brothers/Big Sisters organization. This is also the year they have talked their mother into joining them.

Ready to get wet? Here's some polar bear math:

"It's a cleansing of the soul. You never feel more alive." Stan Braun

1. **Each block cut and heaved from the water measures 36" long x 36" wide x 12" thick. How many cubic inches of ice are in each block?**

2. **If it takes about 9 cubic inches of ice to make a pound, how many pounds does each of the blocks weigh?**

3. **Using metric measurement, each big block is approximately 1 meter long by 1 meter wide by 30 cm thick. What is the volume of one block in cubic centimeters?**

4. **When an ice block melts, it takes up less space. Divide the metric volume of one ice block by 1.1 to find the volume of water it contains.** Round to nearest whole cubic centimeter.

5. **Find the difference between the volume of a frozen block of ice and the melted block.**

6. **The total swimming area that is cut from the ice is 30 feet long by 10 feet wide. Each participant jumps into the shallow end, where the water is 4½ feet deep, and swims toward the deep end, where it is 18 feet deep. In the freezing water, muscles tighten and barely move. A swimmer is lucky to go even 2 feet with each stroke.**

How many strokes would a good swimmer need to get across to the other side?

Want to know what it feels like to polar bear swim?

- As you plunge into icy water, all your body systems are put on alert.
- Your body registers intense pain.
- The blood vessels in your skin and fingers constrict. Numbness sets in.

- Your blood pressure rises, and your heart races.
- Your muscles tense and cramp.
- Fear hormones are released, causing panic.
- Your heart and breathing stops momentarily.
- You gasp for air.

If the swim was much longer:
- Your consciousness would cloud.
- You would be dazed and irrational; you might even stop trying to get to safety.
- You would freeze to death. Even a few degrees change in your core temperature can be fatal.

Connie, Stan, and Scott do their polar bear swimming close to shore, with trained paramedics and emergency equipment standing guard. Only in these controlled conditions can the risks be said to balance with the thrills.

Sources:

Piven, J., & Borgenicht, D. (2001). *Worst-case scenario survival handbook: Travel.* San Francisco: Chronicle Books.

Pozos, R., & Born, D. (1982). *Hypothermia—causes, effects, prevention.* Petaluma, CA: New Century Publishers.

Carol & Joe Shields
Scuba Divers

Converting hours to minutes and back again
Multiplying and dividing fractions
Converting improper fractions to mixed numbers
Finding a pattern

As certified SCUBA (self-contained underwater breathing apparatus) diving instructors, Carol and Joe Shields have dived hundreds of feet deep, investigated sunken shipwrecks, explored underwater caverns, recovered submerged bodies, and probed the mysterious world underneath ice floes. In the last 20 years, they have taught more than 600 people to scuba dive. Besides teaching scuba diving, Joe and Carol are college professors of mathematics and computer science. In their own words:

"There's plenty of mathematics involved in scuba diving, and it's the kind that will save your life. Here's an example:

"Fresh water weighs 62.4 pounds per cubic foot and salt water weighs 64 pounds per cubic foot. All that weight above your head is the pressure you feel underwater, and it can cause problems.

"On land, we experience one atmosphere (1 atm) of pressure, which is the weight of all the air above us, and that alone is 14.7 pounds of pressure on each square inch of our bodies. We don't feel that pressure because we are so used to it. Now it has been calculated that 33 feet of water weighs the same as the entire air above a person. So, when you dive 33 feet under water, you're really experiencing two atmospheres—29.4 pounds per square inch (14.7 pounds per square inch times two).

At 66 feet, you're experiencing three atmospheres, or 44.1 pounds on every square inch of your body.

"Because of the intense increase in pressure as you descend, you can't just go shooting up to the surface when you run out of air. You need to give your body time to decompress, like opening a can of soda slowly. Decompression may take several minutes, and you don't want to run out of air, so you'd better know for sure how long your tank will last even before you dive in. You will need to figure that you will use more air when the water is colder and (here's where the math comes in) at greater depths.

"You need 1 atmosphere of air at the surface. In order to fill your lungs when you are 33 feet underwater, you need to breathe in twice as many air molecules as you would breathe at the surface. At 66 feet, you need to breathe in three times as many. Each additional 33 feet of salt water requires another atmosphere of air to fill our lungs. So, at 33 feet, your tank will last half as long as it would at the surface, and at 66 feet, one-third as long. Can you see why that's important?"

1. **If your tank will last one hour at the surface, how long will it last at 66 feet?** (Hint: Draw yourself a chart. You'll want to use it to solve the other problems as well.)

2. **How long will it last at 99 feet?**

3. **A standard aluminum tank contains 80 cubic feet of air when full and will normally last 1 hour and 20 minutes on the surface, depending on the individual.**

   How long will it last at 55 feet? Hint #1: 55 feet = 2 ATM + how many ATMs? Hint #2 (if you need it): 55 feet = $2\frac{22}{33}$ ATMs

4. **Suppose your tank lasts 25 minutes at 77 feet. How long would it have lasted at the surface?** Find to the nearest hour and minute. Hint: It would have lasted longer.

5. **A diver at 77 feet finds that her tank will last 20 minutes. How long would that same tank have lasted at 33 feet?** Hint: First, find how long it would have lasted at the surface. When you get the answer, round to the nearest minute.

6. **"Exploring shipwrecks is an adrenaline rush," Joe says, "and when people are anxious or excited or working very hard, they breathe a lot faster and use more air."**

   Suppose your tank will last you 75 minutes when you are at the surface and calm, but you find it only lasts 15 minutes when exploring your first shipwreck at 66 feet underwater.

   How many times more air did you consume than you would have if you had been calm?

Joe will never forget the time he was exploring a sunken wooden schooner on the bottom of Lake Huron. The wreck suddenly shifted, and the ship's floor caved in on top of him! He was trapped 86 feet down. After a long search, Joe was able to find a small hole, but too small to fit through. Joe removed his air tank and was able to barely squeeze through.

Another time, Carol and Joe were videotaping moray eels in Honduras, when an eel suddenly clamped onto another diver and wouldn't let go. Joe and Carol pulled the diver to the surface and whacked off the eel with a knife in order to save the diver's life.

Even with eels, collapsing shipwrecks, equipment failure, and sharks, the Shields say diving is one of the safer extreme sports. "In most scuba diving accidents, human error is the cause … which means the accidents could have been prevented."

9 Erik Weihenmayer
Mountain Climber

Multistep problem solving
Finding rate using division
Finding percentages
Conversions, approximate
Large number division

Approximately 90% of the highly skilled mountain climbers who attempt to climb Mount Everest never reach the summit. For every eight people who do reach it, one person dies trying. Erik Weihenmayer reached the top of Mount Everest, and, even more important, he made it back alive. You may be interested to know that Erik Weihenmayer is totally blind.

Erik was legally blind at birth and lost his vision completely by age 13, but that didn't stop him from scrambling up his first rock face at the age of 16. Sitting on the ledge well above the tree line, Erik could feel the texture of the rocks under his hands and the warm sun on his face and the sense of openness all around him. "It was then that I knew that I would never drive a car in the Indy 500 or catch a ball in the World Series—but I could climb mountains," says Erik. "I came to know that blindness would often be a nuisance, would sometimes make my life more difficult, but would never be a barrier in my path."

High-altitude mountain climbing is one of the hardest physical activities a person can do. Mountain

"Blindness is this incredible adventure that presents me with exciting challenges every day of my life." Erik Weihenmayer

climbing often involves days, even months, of continual stress from exertion and exposure. Gusts on the mountain may blow 100 miles an hour. Perched in

"Often, we are forced to throw out the expectations of others and simply rise to the level of our own internal potential." Erik Weihenmayer

these winds at an angle on a sheer rock face with the thermometer reading 50 degrees below zero, sleep is impossible. Worst of all for the high-altitude climber is the lack of oxygen, which causes headaches, fever, nausea, vomiting, irrational thinking, and confusion.

To attempt to climb Everest, therefore, is to accept the very real possibility of death. Sometimes, the climber is overpowered by an avalanche and asphyxiates under a mountain of snow. Sometimes, a climber falls into a crevasse and there awaits death by freezing. Sometimes, a climber's brain will burst from lack of oxygen. At least 165 people have died on Mount Everest in the last 50 years. Erik knew his training and skills were sufficient to make the climb, so he decided to go for it. He planned to find his way by following a bell suspended from his teammate's pole, and the teammates would shout directions as needed. Many elite climbers cautioned Erik not to attempt Everest. But, Erik was used to people telling him what he could not do, and he knew that sometimes you just have to go for it.

"In order to climb Mt. Everest safely, I needed to get used to the lack of oxygen at higher elevations slowly. This process is called acclimatizing. My plan was to climb from Base Camp to Camp 1 and back three times, then climb from Base Camp to Camp 2

"There's definitely physics involved, and math. You're constantly assessing spaces and asking yourself, 'Are our ropes long enough to reach up to the anchor and back down to the next climber?'" Erik Weihenmayer

and back once, then climb from Base Camp to Camp 4 and back once, and then descend from Base Camp to the little village of Dingboche at 14,000 feet to rest for a few days before the 4-day climb to the summit and final descent to Base Camp."

Approximate Elevations

Summit:	29,035'
Camp 4:	26,000'
Camp 3:	24,000'
Camp 2:	22,000'
Camp 1:	20,000'
Base Camp:	18,000'

1. How many feet of elevation (gain plus loss) did Erik plan to cover?

Sound easy? Erik's first climb from Base Camp to Camp 1 took 13 hours. He was bloody and green from altitude sickness when he arrived at Camp 1, but he refused to quit. He climbed back down to Base Camp, and as soon as he was able, did it again. By the final time, Erik had cut his time to only 5 hours.

2. What was Erik's rate of ascent from Base Camp to Camp 1 the first time he ascended?

Find answer in feet per hour.

3. What was his rate of ascent from Base Camp to Camp 1 the final time he ascended?

On the final summit push from Camp 4, Erik's team ran into treacherous winds on top of perilous ice. Approaching the Balcony (27,500'), the team also had to deal with driving snow and lightning crashing around them. They huddled to decide whether to continue upward. A forecast from Base Camp of clear skies ahead urged them on.

Finally, Erik and his companions stood on the south summit (28,750'), which has a 10,000-foot vertical fall into the country of Tibet on one side and a 7,000-foot vertical fall into the country of Nepal on the other. But, Everest's highest peak still lay ahead. The team climbed up the knife-edge ridge to Hillary Step and on to the highest peak of Everest. Erik could tell he had reached the top because, as he described it, "the sound vibrations are so different." Erik and his companions were standing on the top of the world.

4.   How much higher is the highest summit than the south summit?

Climbers wear a harness attached to a safety rope in case they fall. The lead climber goes up with a rope hanging down behind her, placing anchors in the rock as he climbs. The rope runs through these anchors and down to the climbing partner below. The climber below (called the belay) holds the rope tightly. If the lead climber should fall, the rope and the anchor will catch her.

Climbing is never easy, particularly because the lead climber must climb above the protection of the last anchor in order to place the next one. If the lead climber, Sydney, should fall when she is 5 meters above the last anchor, she would actually fall at least 10 meters.

5.   Why?

The fall factor refers to how much the fall is going to hurt. The fall factor is found by dividing the length of the fall by the length of rope between the belayer and the lead climber. Sydney had climbed 40 meters above the belayer when she fell.

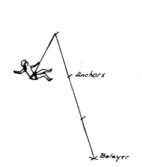

6.   What was the fall factor of Sydney's fall? (The fall factor is shown as a decimal.)

Fall factors 1 and above can cause serious injury. If Sydney hadn't placed any anchors for protection, she would have fallen all the way to the end of her rope, below the belayer.

7.   What would the fall factor have been if Sydney had not placed any anchors?

Climbing rope stretches to take some of the shock from a fall.

Avalanches are one of the leading causes of death on Everest. You can't outrun an avalanche. An avalanche can zoom down a mountain at 200 miles per hour.

Erik says, "Here's a problem I have encountered. I am at 6,800 meters above sea level on my third day of climbing Ama Dablam, one of the steepest and most beautiful mountains in the world. Temperature with wind chill is 3 degrees below zero.

> **"Success is not just the crowning moment, the spiking of the ball in the end zone, or the raising of the flag on the summit. It is the whole process of reaching for a goal, and sometimes it begins with failure."**
> Erik Weihenmayer

I have just climbed straight up from where the belayer is holding the rope below. I have been screwing metal anchors into the ice every 10 vertical feet. Just as I am about to place the fifth anchor, the chunk of ice my tools are gripping breaks loose and I plunge downward. Good thing that fourth anchor is securely placed! I know that the rope will stretch 10% of its length from the hands of the belayer through the four anchors to where it is attached to my harness."

8. How far will Erik fall before the rope stops him?

9. What would be the fall factor of this fall?

So, you've decided to take up rock climbing! Be sure to learn from competent professionals. One thing they will teach you is about ropes. A single rope (11 millimeters in diameter) has a breaking strength of 2,300 kilograms. That means it should be able to hold up to 2,300 kg before it breaks.

However, knots cause a decrease in strength of up to 45% depending on the knot used. Running a rope over an edge also causes a loss of strength, by about 30% when it runs over a karabiner. The sharper the edge, the greater the loss that will result. If the rope gets wet or frozen, there will also be a significant loss of strength.

Okay, you've got a new single rope. The label says it holds up to 2,300 kg. You will need to make one knot attaching the rope to you, reducing the strength by 45%.

10. How much will the rope hold now?

You run this same rope through a karabiner and back, reducing the strength another 30%.

11. How many kilograms will the rope be expected to hold now?

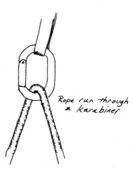

Rope run through a karabiner

Let's say you weigh 150 pounds with all your gear (helmet, karabiners, extra rope, anchors, climbing axe, water bottle, etc.).

12. Can you expect the rope, with one knot, run through one karabiner, to hold you? (Hint #2: You should be able to figure this one out without doing any calculations.)

Besides being the first blind person to ever climb Everest, Erik is also the first blind person ever to climb the Seven Summits, the highest peaks on each of the seven continents. Very few people in the world have climbed what Erik has climbed:

North America's Denali Alaska, 20,320'—Erik climbed it in 1995. He was snowed in a pup tent on a 3-foot-wide ice shelf near the summit for a week.

Africa's Mt. Kilimanjaro Tanzania, 19,341'—Erik summited Kilamanjaro in 1997. He and his wife Ellen were married high on the slopes of this mountain.

South America's Aconcagua Argentina, 22,841'—Aconcagua is the highest mountain in the Western Hemisphere. Erik climbed it in 1999.

Antarctica's Vinson Massif 16,067'—Vinson Massif lies in the least habitable region on Earth. Erik climbed it in 2001.

Asia's Everest Nepal and Tibet, 29,035'—Erik climbed Everest in 2002. Everest is known as *Chomolungma*, which means "Goddess Mother of the Earth" in Tibetan.

Europe's Mt. Elbrus Russia 18,510'—Erik climbed Elbrus in 2002, and descended much of the way on skis!

Australia's Mount Kosciuszko 7,316'—Erik climbed Mount Kosciuszko in 2002.

13. What is the average height of all seven mountains in miles? Round to the nearest mile. Hint: one mile equals 5,280 feet.

"Everyone needs a vision. A vision is deeper than a goal, more complex. It's where all your goals spring from. It's how we see ourselves living our lives, serving other people; and what kind of legacy we want to leave behind."

Climbing as a metaphor for life: "Imagine everyone connected by a giant rope, helping each other, compensating for individual weaknesses, using everyone's abilities to the fullest." Erik Weihenmayer

Climbing Everest is only one of many high points Erik has experienced. He is also an acrobatic skydiver and skier, a long-distance biker and marathoner, a wrestler and scuba diver, a lecturer, an author, a middle school teacher, a husband, and a father. To Weihenmayer, playing with his baby daughter is a high point like Everest.

"There are summits everywhere. You just have to know where to look."

Sources

Weihenmayer, E. (2002). *Touch the top of the world*. New York: Plume.

For speaking engagements: Ed Weihenmayer at (904) 321-1938 or by e-mail at tigertops@net-magic.net.

For corporate events: Leading Authorities at (202) 783-0300
For media: Daphne Hoyft, Cohn, & Wolfe at (212) 798-9519

Visit Erik Weihenmayer's Web site at http://www. touchthetop.com.

Additional Sources

Greenfield, K. T. (2001, June 18). "Blind to Failure." *Time, 157*(24), 52–64.

Weihenmayer, E. (2001, December). "Tenacious E." *Outside,* 54.

Fyffe, A., & Peter I. (1997). *The handbook of climbing.* New York: Penguin.

ANSWERS

7 E. J. Jackson: Freestyle Kayaker

1. **What's the multiplier?**

Throw out the high (15) and the low (7), and add the remaining two scores (10 + 10). **The multiplier is 20.**

2. **Find the Variety Points score.**

Throw out 1; throw out 5.
The average of 2 and 3 is 2.5.
Then add 1.

2.5 + 1 = **3.5**

3. **Now multiply the Technical Score times the Variety Points.**

```
    3.5
x   2 0
    0 0
   70 0
   70.0 = 70
```

4. **Discarding the high and low, what was your average?**

Discard 7 and 13.
The average of 8 and 10 is **9.**

5. **Take that % of 70.**

```
   70
x .09
 6.30
```
6.3 style bonus points

6. **Add this to the previous answer to get your total score.**

$$\begin{array}{r} 70.0 \\ +\ \underline{6.3} \\ 76.3 \end{array}$$ **76.3** You won!

David Casarotto: Skydiver

1. **Look at the table below. How far has David fallen in the first second?**

Time Since Leaving Plane	Total Length of All
1 second	16 feet
2 seconds	62 feet
3 seconds	138 feet
6 seconds	500 feet
9 seconds	1028 feet
12 seconds	1556 feet
15 seconds	2084 feet

16 seconds

2. **How far did David fall between the first second and the second second?**

62–16 = **46 feet**

3. **How far did he fall in the first nine seconds?**

1028 feet

4　**How many miles are you falling every minute?**

120 mi per hr = 120 mi per 60 min
120 mi/60 min = X mi/1 min
120 mi/60 min = 2 mi per min

2 miles per minute

5.　**How many seconds will it take you to fall 1 mile?**

2 mi/1 min = 1 mi/X min
Cross multiply.
2X = 1
X = ½ min

X = 30 seconds

6.　**How many feet are you falling each second?**
(Hint: There are 5,280 feet in a mile.)

$$\frac{5280 \text{ ft}}{30 \text{ sec}} = \frac{X \text{ ft}}{1 \text{ sec}}$$

Cross multiply.

(5280)(1) = 30 X

Solve for X.

```
        1 7 6
30 ) 5 2 8 0
     3
     2 2
     2 1
       1 8
       1 8
       0 0
```

X = 176 feet per second

7. How many seconds will it take you to fall 1 mile?

240 mph = 240 mi/60 min

240 mi/60 min= 4 mi/min

4 mi/60 sec =1 mile/15 sec = 5280 ft / 15sec

352 ft per sec

That's over the length of a football field in only 1 second!

8. How much weight is David experiencing?

10 (180 + 20 + 5) = 10 (205) = **2050 pounds**

That's a little over a ton!

9. How many seconds does David have after deployment of the raspberry parachute until he hits the ground?

25 ft/sec
3000/25 = **120 sec**

10. How many seconds does David have after deployment of the lime green parachute until he hits the ground?

40 ft/sec
3000/40 = **75 sec**

ANSWERS

11. David is freefalling in a group at 165 feet per second. At 4,000 feet, he hears the altimeter warn him to break off soon. About how many seconds until he reaches 3,000 feet, when he must deploy his parachute?

1,000 feet/ 165 ft per sec = **about 6 sec**

12. If the temperature on the ground was a pleasant 50 degrees Fahrenheit, what was the temperature up there (not counting wind chill)?

18,000/1,000 = 18

18 x 3 = 54 degree drop in temperature

50–54 = **-4 degrees F**

James Cole: Bronco Rider

1. How much does he win?

50.00	$43.00	$40.00		$800.00	$900.00
- 7.00	- 3.00	x 20 contestants		+ 100.00	x .60
$ 43.00	$40.00	$800.00		$900.00	$540.00

$540

2. How much does each put in for gas?

250 miles divided by 32 miles per gallon = 7.8125 gallons

7.8 gallons times $1.70 per gallon = $13.26

$13.26 divided by 4 guys = **approximately $3.32 each**

3.　Who won each go?

Contestant	First Go	Second Go	Short Go	TOTAL
Tornado Joe	58 – 3 pts	62 – 8 pts	68 – 7 pts	18 pts
Danny Daniels	68 – 7 pts	60 – 7 pts	58 – 5 pts	19 pts
Wild Willy	70 – 9 pts	52 – 4 pts	56 – 4 pts	17 pts
Jamers	65 – 5 pts	**70 – 10 pts**	69 – 8 pts	**23 pts**
Oscar	64 – 4 pts	56 – 6 pts	70 – 9 pts	19 pts
Blaze	**72 – 10 pts**	66 – 9 pts	54 – 3 pts	22 pts
Goose-Egg	69 – 8 pts	50 – 3 pts	**72 – 10 pts**	21 pts
Tarzan	67 – 6 pts	54 – 5 pts	67 – 6 pts	17 pts

Winner of First Go: Blaze
Winner of Second Go: Jamers
Winner of Short Go: Goose Egg

4.　Who won overall?

Overall Winner: Jamers, with 23 points

ANSWERS

Juli Lynch: Adventure Racer

1. **In an adventure race, how many calories might you need each hour?**

```
        416.6
24 | 10000
     96
     40
     24
     160
     144
      16
```

417 calories per hour

2. **How many carbohydrate calories will you consume in a full-speed race day?**

10,000 x 0.75 = **7,500 calories**

3. **How many grams of carbohydrates should we take with us per person per day? Think: There will be fewer grams than calories, so our answer will be smaller. Therefore, we should divide.**

```
     1875
4 | 7500
    4
    35
    32
    30
    28
    20
    20
     0
```

4.   If you weigh 100 pounds, what is your weight to the nearest kilogram?

100 x 0.45 = 45.00 = **45 kilograms**

5.   How many grams of protein would you need to take for each day of the race if you weigh 100 pounds?

```
      4 5
x     1.6
      270
       45
      72.0
```

72 grams

6.   If you need to eat 1,000 calories of fat each day of a 6-day race, how many grams of fat should you pack?

1,000 calories x 6 days = 6,000 calories

```
       666.6
   9 ) 6000.0
        54
        60
```

667 grams (or 666 if you rounded earlier)

7.   Estimated Distance of Route A:

Measuring with a string and comparing it to the scale, you get close to **40 km.**

8.   Estimated Distance of Route B:

Approximately 60 km

9. **Estimated Distance of Route C:**

Approximately 50 km

10. **How long will it take to complete Route A?**

40K/8K per hour = **5 hours**

11. **How long will it take to complete Route B?**

60/8 = **7½ hours**

12. **How long will it take to complete Route C?**

50/8 = 6.25 = **6½ hours**

13. **Elevation gain of Route A:**

17 contour lines = **1,700 meters**

14. **Elevation gain of Route B:**

4 contour lines = **400 meters**

15. **Elevation Gain of Route C:**

7 contour lines = **700 meters**

16. **Hours to complete Route A considering elevation gain.**

Think: How many 300s in 1,700? Well, let's divide and see.

$$\frac{5.67}{300 \overline{)1700}}$$

$$\underline{1500}$$

200   Remainder is closer to 150 (half) than to 300 (whole), so round to nearest half.

5½ hours added due to elevation

5 hours (see answer #10) plus 5½ hours = **10½ hours total**

17. Hours to complete Route B considering elevation gain.

$$\frac{1.3}{300 \overline{)400.0}} \text{ meters}$$

$$\underline{300}$$

$$1000$$

$$\underline{900}$$

100   Remainder is close to 150 (half).

1½ hours + 7½ hours = **9 hours**

18. Hours to complete Route C considering elevation gain.

$$\frac{2.3}{300 \overline{)700.0}} \text{ meters}$$

$$\underline{600}$$

$$1000$$

$$\underline{900}$$

$$100$$

2½ hours + 6½ hours = **9 hours**

Jamie Simon: Freestyle Kayaker

1. Help Jamie calculate the average drop of the rest of the route.

Start by writing down what you know: 7 miles drops 2,750 feet, but one of these miles drops 500 feet. Therefore, 6 miles drop 2,750–500 = 2,250 feet.

```
       375  feet per mile
  6 ) 2250
      18
      45
      42
      30
      30
```

375 feet per mile

2. How many feet high is Hollin Falls?

The question is:	15.5 meters = how many feet
We know:	1 yard = 0.914 meters
Therefore:	3 feet = 0.914 meters

So then: What part of a meter does 1 foot equal?

Divide:
```
      .304
  3 ) 0.914
      9
      10
      014
      12
```
Therefore, 1 foot = approximately 0.3 meters

How many times can .3 meters go into 15.5 meters?

```
       5 1
  .3 ) 15.5
       15
        5
        3
```

Hollin Falls is about 51 feet tall.

3. **How many times taller is Hollin Falls than the ceiling in this room?**

Most ceilings are 10 feet tall.

$$10\overline{)51} ^{5}$$

$$\underline{50}$$

$$1$$

Hollin falls is about FIVE times taller than most ceilings. (Hollin Falls is as high as a five-story building).

Jeff Gildehaus: Hang Glider

1. **Prepare a chart comparing statistics on the two hang gliders:**

Name of Glider	Sail Area	Glide Ratio	Sink Rate	Stall Speed	Max Speed
Fletcher	160 sq ft	4:01	250 ft/min	15 mph	35 mph
Barney	147 sq ft	13:01	170 ft/min	17 mph	50 mph

2. **If I were to take off from a cliff with 1,000 ft. of vertical between the launch and the landing area in my first hang glider, Fletcher, and then in my current hang glider, Barney, how much farther would I glide flying Barney?**

Fletcher traveled 4 feet for every 1 foot of drop,
So it traveled 4,000 feet for every 1,000 feet of drop.

Barney travels 13 feet for every 1 foot of drop,
So it travels 13,000 feet for every 1,000 feet of drop.

13,000 ft–4,000 ft = **9,000 ft farther**

3. **How long would I be able to stay in the air with Fletcher assuming there was no wind to extend the flight?**

Fletcher had a sink rate of 250 feet per minute, so it will drop 1,000 feet in how many minutes?

1,000 feet divided by 250 feet per minute = **4 minutes**

4. **How long would I be able to stay in the air with Barney assuming there was no wind to extend the flight?** (Round to the nearest whole number.)

Barney has a sink rate of 170 ft./min, so it will drop 1,000 feet in how many minutes?

```
          5.8
170 )1000.0
     850
     1500
     1360
      140
```

6 minutes

5. **Draw a line on the chart showing my approx-imate elevation over the first 20 minutes.**

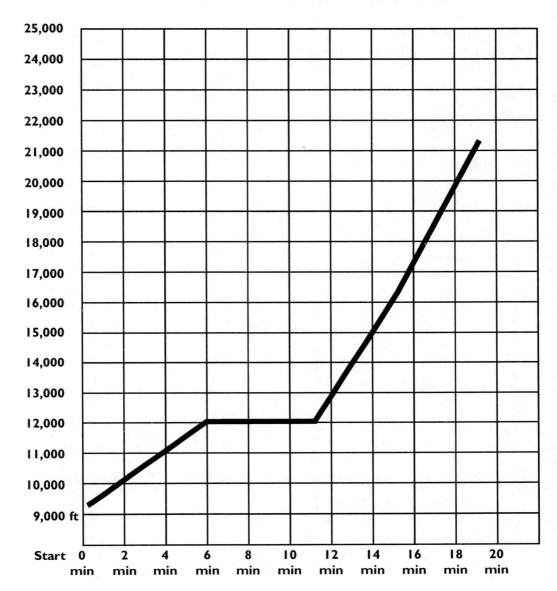

6. **What was my rate of climb the first 6 min-utes of the flight?**

The first 6 minutes Jeff rose from 9,000 to 12,000 feet.
12,000 – 9,000 = 3,000 feet of elevation gain
3,000 divided by 6 min. =

500 feet/minute

7. What was my rate of climb from 11 minutes to 19 minutes? (Round to the nearest whole number.)

Jeff went from 12,000 feet to 21, 500 feet.
Subtract to find the difference:

```
   21,500
 − 12,000
    9,500 feet difference
```

It took him 8 minutes, so:

```
        1187.5
  8 ) 9500.0
     8
     15
      8
     70
     64
      60
      56
       40
       40
```

1,188 feet/minute

8. How much longer was Manfred's flight distance than mine?

435 miles–100 miles = **335 miles longer**

9. How much longer was Manfred's flight time than mine?

```
     10 hours 30 minutes = 9 hours 90 minutes
 −    4 hours 45 minutes = 4 hours 45 minutes
                           5 hours 45 minutes
```

5 hours 45 minutes longer

10. **What was my average speed over the ground on my cross-country flight? (Don't count the first 45 minutes of circling.)**

(4 hours 45 minutes)–(45 minutes) = 4 hours.
I went 100 miles in 4 hours.
How far did I go in one hour?
100 divided by 4 = 25 miles per hour

average speed of 25 mph

11. **What was Manfred's average speed to the nearest whole number?**

```
        41.4
10.5 |435.00  miles
     420
      15 0
      10 5
       4 50
       4 20
         30
```

41 miles per hour

12. **About how many hours would it have taken me to get home if I had been able to fly as fast as Manfred Ruhmer?**

```
          3.1
41 mph |131.00  miles
       123
         8 0
         4 1
         3 9
```

3 hours

The Braun Family: Polar Bear Swimmers

1. How many cubic inches of ice are in each block?

12 x 36 x 36 = **15,552 cubic inches**

2. How many pounds does each one of the big blocks weigh?

15,552 divided by 9 = **1,728 pounds**

3. What is the volume of each block in cubic centimeters?

100 cm x 100 cm x 30 cm = **300,000 cubic centimeters**

4. Divide the volume of one ice block by 1.1 to find out how many cubic centimeters of water it contains.

300,000/1.1 = 272,727.2727 = **272,727 cubic centimeters**

5. Find the difference between the volume of the frozen block of ice and the melted block.

300,000 − 272,727 = **27,273 cubic centimeters**

6. How many strokes would a good swimmer need to get across to the other side? More information than you need was given.

The answer is found by dividing 30 feet by 2 = **15 strokes**

Carol & Joe Shields: Scuba Divers

1. **If our tank will last an hour on the surface, how long will it last at 66 feet?** (Hint: Draw yourself a chart showing the number of atmospheres of pressure at each depth (multiples of 33).)

DEPTH	ATMS
Sea Level	1
33 ft	2
66 ft	3
99 ft	4
132 ft	5
165 ft	6

60 minutes ÷ 3 atmospheres = **20 minutes**

2. **How long will it last at 99 feet?**

60 minutes ÷ 4 atmospheres = **15 minutes**

3. **How long will it last at 55 feet?**

Since atm change every 33 feet,
55 feet = 33 feet + 22 feet
$^{22}/_{33}$ = ⅔ atm of water pressure
55 feet = 1⅔ atm
Now add 1 atm for air pressure at the surface (0 feet) = 2⅔ atmospheres

80 ÷ 2⅔ = 80 ÷ ⁸⁄₃ = 80 x ⅜ = **30 minutes**

4. **Suppose that your tank lasts 25 minutes at 77 feet. How long would it have lasted at the surface?**

$77 \div 33 = 2\frac{1}{3}$ atm, then add 1 for the surface air pressure $= 3\frac{1}{3}$ atmospheres

25 minutes x $3\frac{1}{3}$ atmospheres = 25 x $^{10}\!/_3$ = $^{250}\!/_3$ = about 83 minutes

83 minutes = **1 hour 23 minutes**

5. **A diver at 77 feet finds that her tank will last 20 minutes. How long would that same tank have lasted at 33 feet?** (Hint: First find how long would it have lasted at the surface.)

In problem #4 we found that 77 feet = $3\frac{1}{3}$ atmospheres

We know it would have lasted longer at the surface, so we multiply.

$3\frac{1}{3}$ x 20 = 67 minutes at the surface

We know 33 feet = 2 atmospheres

$67 \div 2 =$ **approximately 33 minutes**

6. **How many times more air did you consume than you would have if you had been calm?**

Start by writing what you know:

It lasted 75 minutes at 1 atmosphere.

66 feet = 3 atmospheres

75 minutes ÷ 3 = 25 minutes

It would have lasted 25 minutes if you were calm.

It only lasted 15 minutes.

25 compares to 15 as: $^{25}\!/_{15} =$ **$1\frac{2}{3}$ times more air**

Erik Weihenmayer: Mountain Climber

1. How many feet of elevation gain/loss did I plan to climb?

Approximate Elevations:
Dingboche: 14,000'
Base Camp: 18,000'
Camp 1:   20,000'
Camp 2:   22,000'
Camp 3:   24,000'
Camp 4:   26,000'
Summit: 29,035'

Base Camp to Camp 1:
2,000 feet x 2 (round trip) x 3 (times) = 12,000 feet

Base Camp to Camp 2:
4,000 feet x 2 (round trip) x 1 (time) = 8,000 feet

Base Camp to Camp 4:
26,000 – 18,000 = 8,000 feet
8,000 feet x 2 (round trip) x 1 (time) = 16,000 feet

Base Camp to Dingboche:
4,000 feet x 2 (round trip) x 1 (time) = 8,000 feet

Base Camp to Summit:
29,035 – 18,000 = 11,035 feet
11,035 x 2 (round trip) x 1 (time) = 22,070 feet

Add them together:

```
     12,000
      8,000
     16,000
      8,000
 +   22,070
     66,070
```

66,070 feet

ANSWERS

2. What was Erik's rate of ascent from Base Camp to Camp 1 the first time he ascended?

2,000 feet in 13 hours = how many feet in 1 hour?

2,000 / 13 = x / 1

```
        153.8
13 ⟌ 2000.0
     13
      70
      65
       50
       39
      110
      104
        6
```

154 feet per hour

3. What was his rate of ascent from Base Camp to Camp 1 the final time he tried it?

2000 feet divided by 5 hours = **400 feet per hour**

4. How much higher is the highest summit than the South Summit?

Summit 29,035 – South Summit 28,750 = **285 feet higher**

5. Why?

The lead climber will drop twice the distance that he was above the last anchor. In this case, Sydney falls 5 meters to the anchor, then another 5 meters below it, for a total of 10 meters.

10 meters

ANSWERS

6. What was the fall factor of Sydney's fall?

length of fall 10 m/length of rope 40 m = **fall factor of 0.25**

7. What would the fall factor have been if Sydney hadn't placed any anchors?

In the worst-case scenario, Sydney would have fallen 40 m to the belayer and then an additional 40 m below the belayer, for an 80 meter fall.

There was only 40 meters of rope from the belayer to Sydney.

length of fall 80 meters/length of rope 40 meters = **2**

fall factor of 2

8. How far will I fall before the rope stops me?

Start by writing down what you know, and drawing a diagram if it helps.

50 feet of rope	Erik will fall 10 feet to the anchor
x .10	+ 10 feet below the anchor
5.00 feet of stretch	+ 5 feet stretch
	Total: 25 feet

25 feet

9. What would be the fall factor of this fall?

Length of fall 25/length of rope 50 = $^{25}\!/_{50}$ = ½

½ = **0.5**

10. How much will the rope hold now?

100% − 45% reduced = it will be able to hold 55% of 2300 kg

2,300 kg x 0.55 = **1,265 kg**

11. How many kilograms would the rope hold now?

If the rope will be reduced by 30%, it will be able to hold 70% of what it could.

Therefore, it can hold

$$
\begin{array}{r}
1265.00 \\
\times \quad\quad .70 \\
\hline
885.50
\end{array}
$$

885.5 kilograms

12. Can you expect the rope, with one knot, run through one karabiner, to hold you? (Hint: There are 2.2 pounds in every kilogram.)

Ask yourself, "Will the number of kilograms be more or less than 150?" Kilograms are bigger than pounds, so your weight will take fewer kilograms. Since the rope will hold 885 kilograms, it will hold at least 885 pounds.

Yes.

13. What is the average height of all seven mountains in miles?

Denali	20,320'
Mt. Kilimanjaro	19,341'
Aconcagua	22,841'
Mt. Elbrus	18,510'
Everest	29,035'
Vinson Massif	16,067'
Mount Kosciuszko	7,316'
	133,430'

```
                    19,061.4
7 mountains  133,430.0
             7
             6 3
             6 3
               04
                0
               43
               42
               10
                7
               30
               28


                         3.6
5,280 ft per mile  19,061.4
                   15840
                   32214
                   31680
                     534
```

4 miles

Cautionary Note
to the Readers

For the most part, the people highlighted within these pages do not take unnecessary chances.

They are at the top of their fields because they have avoided situations where the risk is too high and the chance of injury is too great.

They know it is better to walk away from a risk with all your faculties intact than to plunge forward and possibly lose everything.

So be wise ... enjoy life ... and take care.

Kip & Marya Tyler
Authors

Even as Kip and Marya were deciding to collaborate on a mathematics book about extreme sports, they were falling in love, and this book is the offspring of their continued love for each other. They met while Kip was wilderness crew leader for the U.S. Forest Service in Montana; Marya arrived as a volunteer.

Back in 1983, Kip left his fast-paced management job in the auto industry and ventured west. Since then, he has fought forest fires, patrolled the backcountry on skis and horseback, explored technical mountain faces, built trails, and maintained remote cabins for the Forest Service in Oregon, Montana, Wyoming, California, and Alaska. Marya loves the outdoors, has a master's degree in education, and has been a schoolteacher of gifted and talented children for 11 years. She has four gifted children of her own, and this book is dedicated to them and to all who find adventure in learning.

Kip and Marya Tyler
P.O. Box 6843
Ketchikan, AK 99901
tyler@kpunet.net

Other books by the authors:

Bollow, N., Berg, R., & Tyler, M. (2001). *Alien math*. Waco, TX: Prufrock Press.

Kleiman, A., Washington, D., & Washington, M. F. (1996). *It's alive!* Waco, TX: Prufrock Press.

Kleiman, A., Washington, D., & Washington, M. F. (1996). *It's alive … and kicking*. Waco, TX: Prufrock Press.

Tyler, M. W. (1995). *Real life math mysteries*. Waco, TX: Prufrock Press.